GOD'S WORD REMAINS

PROVERBS & POWERFUL PRAYERS
FOR SPIRITUAL & FINANCIAL BREAKTHROUGH

Lissa Thomas

Divine Works Publishing
Royal Palm Beach, Florida

© 2025 Lissa Thomas

All Rights Reserved. No part of this publication may be reproduced, stored in a retrieval system, or transmitted in any form or by any means, electronic, mechanical, photocopying, recording or otherwise without the prior permission of the publisher or in accordance with the provisions of the Copyright, Designs, and Patents Act 1988 or under the terms of any license permitting limited copying issued by the Copyright Licensing Agency.

The views expressed in this work are solely those of the author and do not necessarily reflect the views of the publisher. The publisher hereby disclaims any responsibility for them.

ISBN: 978-1-969860-04-1 (paperback)
ISBN: 978-1-949105-29-2 (eBook)

First Edition Published: 07/25/2025

Sources Cited: Scriptures by King James Version (KJV) unless otherwise noted. **Holy Bible, New Living Translation,** copyright © 1996, 2004, 2015 by Tyndale House Foundation. Used by permission of Tyndale House Publishers, Inc., Carol Stream, Illinois 60188. All Rights Reserved. **Holy Bible, New International Version®, NIV®** Copyright ©1973, 1978, 1984, 2011 by Biblica, Inc.® Used by permission. All Rights Reserved.

Divine Works Publishing books are available at special discounts when purchased in quantity for premiums and promotions and for educational and fundraising use. For details, feel free contact us via email:
books@divineworkspublishing.com or call the number listed below.

Published by:
Divine Works Publishing
Royal Palm Beach, Florida USA
www.DivineWorksPublishing.com
561-990-BOOK (2665)

CONTENTS

Section 1 Proverbs | 1

Section 2 Words of Wisdom | 25

Section 3 Prayers Part 1 - Foundational Prayers | 53

       Prayers Part 2 - Financial Provision | 71

       Prayers Part 3 - Financial Breakthrough | 73

       Prayers Part 4 - Financial Protection | 77

About the Author | 81

1 | PROVERBS

PURPOSE OF PROVERBS:
- **TEACH** wisdom & discipline
- **UNDERSTAND** insights of the wise
- **LIVE** successful lives; being fair, just, doing what is right
- **GIVE** Knowledge & Discernment

1. *Rejoice in the Lord, for He is coming; He is coming to judge the world.*

2. *God will judge the world with justice, the nations with truth.*

3. *Righteousness and justice are the foundation of God's throne.*

4. *God protects the lives of all His godly people.*

5. *Jesus is the sacrifice that atones for our sins—not only our sins, but the sins of all the world.*

6. *Direct your children onto the right path, and when they are older, they will not leave it.*

7. *Choose a good reputation over great riches.*

8. *The horse is prepared for the day of battle, but the victory belongs to the Lord.*

9. *Blessed are those who are generous, because they feed the poor.*

10. *Discipline your children while there is hope; otherwise you will ruin their lives.*

11. A person who gets ahead by oppressing the poor or showering gifts on the rich will end in poverty.

12. Don't rob the poor just because you can, or exploit the needy in court, for the Lord is their defender.

13. Just as the rich rule the poor, so the borrower is servant to the lender.

14. The rich and the poor have this in common: the Lord made them both.

15. No human wisdom or understanding or plan can stand against the Lord.

16. Fools have no interest in understanding; they only want to air their own opinion.

17. The man who finds a wife finds a treasure, and he receives favor from the Lord.

18. The tongue can bring death or life; those who love to talk will reap the consequences.

19. The human spirit can endure a sick body, but who can bear a crushed spirit?

20. The rich think of their wealth as a strong defense; they imagine it to be a high wall of safety.

21. A false witness will not go unpunished, nor will a liar escape.

22. There are friends who destroy each other, but a real friend sticks closer than a brother.

23. Better to be poor and honest than to be dishonest and a fool.

24. People ruin their lives by their own foolishness, and then are angry at the Lord.

25. Wealth makes many friends; poverty drives them all away.

26. If you repay good with evil, evil will never leave your house.

27. Starting a quarrel is like opening a floodgate—so stop before a dispute breaks out.

28. Wrongdoers eagerly listen to gossip, and liars pay close attention to slander.

29. Those who mock the poor insult their Maker; those who rejoice at the misfortune of others will be punished.

30. We may throw the dice,* but the Lord determines how they fall.

31. Unfriendly people care only about themselves; they lash out at common sense.

32. Better to be patient than powerful; better to have self-control than to conquer a city.

33. A troublemaker plants seeds of strife; gossip separates the best of friends.

34. Better to live humble with the poor than to share plunder with the proud.

35. Better a dry crust eaten in peace than a house filled with feasting—and conflict.

36. A truly wise person uses few words; a person with understanding is even-tempered.

37. It is wrong to punish the godly for being good, or to flog leaders for being honest.

38. The poor plead for mercy; the rich answer with insults.

39. Acquitting the guilty and condemning the innocent—both are detestable to the Lord.

40. It is senseless to pay tuition to educate a fool, since he has no heart for learning.

41. A friend is always loyal, and a brother is born to help in time of need.

42. Fear of the Lord leads to life, bringing security and protection from harm.

43. Hot-tempered people must pay the penalty; if you rescue them once, you will have to do it again.

44. If you help the poor, you are lending to the Lord, and He will repay you.

45. Keep the commandments and keep your life; despising them leads to death.

46. If you punish a mocker, the simpleminded will learn a lesson; if you correct the wise, they will be wiser.

47. If you stop listening to instruction, my child, you will turn your back on knowledge.

48. Punishment is made for mockers, and the backs of fools are made to be beaten.

49. Wine produces mockers; alcohol leads to brawls. Those led astray by drink cannot be wise.

50. Sensible people control their temper; they earn respect by overlooking wrongs.

51. The relatives of the poor despise them—how much more will their friends avoid them!

52. Many seek favors from a ruler; everyone is the friend of a person who gives gifts.

53. Many will say they are loyal friends, but who can find one who is truly reliable?

54. Lazy people sleep soundly, but idleness leaves them hungry.

55. Don't say, "I will get even for this wrong." Wait for the Lord to handle the matter.

56. If you insult your father or mother, your light will be snuffed out in total darkness.

57. A gossip goes around telling secrets, so don't hang around with chatterers.

58. Stolen bread tastes sweet, but it turns to gravel in the mouth.

59. If you love to sleep, you will end up in poverty. Keep your eyes open, and there will be plenty to eat.

60. The Lord directs our steps, so why try to understand everything along the way?

61. Don't trap yourself by making a rash promise to God, and only later counting the cost.

62. The Lord's light penetrates the human spirit*, exposing every hidden motive.

63. The glory of the young is their strength; the gray hair of experience is the splendor of the old.

64. People may be right in their own eyes, but the Lord examines their heart.

65. The Lord is more pleased when we do what is right and just than when we offer Him sacrifices.

66. Haughty eyes, a proud heart, and evil actions are all sin.

67. Good planning and hard work lead to prosperity, but hasty shortcuts lead to poverty.

68. Wealth created by a lying tongue is a vanishing mist and a deadly trap.

69. The violence of the wicked sweeps them away, because they refuse to do what is just.

70. Those who shut their ears to the cries of the poor will be ignored in their own time of need.

71. Justice is a joy to the godly, but it terrifies evildoers.

72. The person who strays from common sense will end up in the company of the dead.

73. Ears to hear and eyes to see—both are gifts from the Lord.

74. Even children are known by the way they act—whether their conduct is pure and whether it is right.

75. The godly walk with integrity; blessed are their children who follow them.

76. Who can say, "I have cleansed my heart; I am pure and free from sin"?

77. Whoever pursues righteousness and unfailing love will find life, righteousness, and honor.

78. Some people are always greedy for more, but the godly love to give.

79. Watch your tongue and keep your mouth shut, and you will stay out of trouble.

80. Throw out the mocker, and fighting goes too; quarrels and insults will disappear.

81. While dining with a ruler, pay attention to what is put before you. Don't desire all the delicacies, for he might be trying to trick you.

82. True humility and fear of the Lord lead to riches, honor, and long life.

83. Don't befriend angry people or associate with hot-tempered people, or you will learn to be like them and endanger your soul.

84. A prudent person foresees danger and takes precautions; the simpleton goes blindly on and suffers the consequences.

85. Don't envy sinners, but always continue to fear the Lord. You will be rewarded for this; your hope will not be disappointed.

86. My child,* if your heart is wise, my own heart will rejoice! Everything in me will celebrate when you speak what is right.

87. Don't fail to discipline your children—they won't die if you spank them. Physical discipline may well save them from death.

88. Don't take the land of defenseless orphans, for their Redeemer* is strong; He Himself will bring their charges against you.

89. Don't eat with people who are stingy; don't desire their delicacies. They are always thinking about how much it costs.*

90. Don't rejoice when your enemies fall; don't be happy when they stumble, for the Lord will be displeased with you and will turn His anger away from them.

91. Listen to your father, who gave you life, and don't despise your mother when she is old.

92. The godly may trip seven times, but they will get up again; but one disaster is enough to overthrow the wicked.

93. No one can comprehend the height of heaven, the depth of the earth, or all that goes on in the king's mind.

94. Don't testify against your neighbors without cause; don't lie about them.

95. Do your planning and prepare your fields before building your house.

96. My child, fear the Lord and the king; don't associate with rebels, for disaster will hit them suddenly.

97. A house is built by wisdom and becomes strong through good sense.

98. Get the truth and never sell it; also get wisdom, discipline, and good judgment.

99. Just because you've seen something, don't be in a hurry to go to court, for what will you do in the end if your neighbor deals you a shameful defeat?

100. When arguing with your neighbor, don't betray another person's secret. Others may accuse you of gossip, and you will never again regain your good reputation.

101. A person who promises a gift but doesn't give it is like clouds and wind that bring no rain.

102. Don't visit your neighbors too often, or you will wear out your welcome.

103. Trusting a fool to convey a message is like cutting off one's feet or drinking poison.

104. Telling lies about others is as harmful as hitting them with an ax,

wounding them with a sword, or shooting them with a sharp arrow.

105. Putting confidence in an unreliable person in time of trouble is like chewing with a broken tooth or walking on a lame foot.

106. Don't answer the foolish arguments of fools, or you will become as foolish as they are.

107. It is not good to eat too much honey, and it's not good to seek honor for yourself.

108. If your enemies are hungry, give them food to eat; if they are thirsty, give them water to drink. You will heap burning coals of shame on their head, and the Lord will reward you.

109. If you set a trap for others, you will get caught in it yourself; if you roll a boulder down on others, it will crush you instead.

110. Just as damaging as a madman shooting a deadly weapon is someone who lies to a friend and says, "I was only joking."

111. Interfering in someone else's argument is as foolish as yanking a dog's ears.

112. A little extra sleep, a little more slumber, a little folding of the hands to rest—then poverty will pounce on you like a bandit.

113. It is wrong to show favoritism when passing judgment. A judge who says to the wicked, "You are innocent," will be cursed by many and denounced by the nations.

114. Don't brag about tomorrow, since you don't know what the day will bring.

115. Let someone else praise you, not your own mouth—a stranger, not your own lips.

116. Anger is cruel, and wrath is like a flood, but jealousy is even more dangerous.

117. Wounds from a sincere friend are better than many kisses from an enemy.

118. A quarrelsome wife is as annoying as constant dripping on a rainy day. Stopping her complaints is like trying to stop the wind.

119. Deceitful people cover their hatred with pleasant words, but they're deceiving you. They pretend to be kind, but don't believe them—their hearts are full of many evils.

120. While their hatred may be concealed by trickery, their wrongdoing will be exposed in public.

121. Know the state of your flocks, and put your heart into caring for your herds; for riches don't last forever, and the crown might not be passed to the next generation.

122. Fire tests the purity of silver and gold, but a person is tested by being praised.

123. Just as death and destruction* are never satisfied, so human desire is never satisfied.

124. Young people who obey the law are wise; those with wild friends bring shame to their parents.

125. Greedy people try to get rich quick but don't realize they're headed for poverty.

126. People who conceal their sins will not prosper, but if they confess and turn away from them, they will receive mercy.

127. Those who lead good people along an evil path will fall into their

own trap, but the honest will inherit good things.

128. Income from charging high interest rates will end up in the pocket of someone who is kind to the poor.

129. If a wise person takes a fool to court, there will be ranting and ridicule, but no satisfaction.

130. If you assist a thief, you only hurt yourself. You are sworn to tell the truth, but you dare not testify.

131. Pride ends in humiliation, while humility brings honor.

132. There is more hope for a fool than for someone who speaks without thinking.

133. Some people curse their father and do not thank their mother. They are pure in their own eyes, but they are filthy and unwashed.

134. Every word of God proves true; He is a shield to all who come to Him for protection. Do not add to His words, or He may rebuke you and expose you as a liar.

135. If a ruler pays attention to liars, all his advisers will be wicked.

136. As the beating of cream yields butter, and striking the nose causes bleeding, so stirring up anger causes quarrels.

137. The eye that mocks a father and despises a mother's instructions will be plucked out by ravens of the valley and eaten by vultures.

138. If you have been a fool by being proud or plotting evil, cover your mouth in shame.

139. Who can find a virtuous and capable wife? She is more precious than rubies. Her husband can trust her, and she will greatly enrich his life. She brings him good, not harm, all the days of her life.

140. The wicked are trapped by their own words, but the godly escape such trouble.

141. A fool is quick-tempered, but a wise person stays calm when insulted.

142. Truthful words stand the test of time, but lies are soon exposed.

143. The wise don't make a show of their knowledge, but fools broadcast their foolishness.

144. Worry weighs a person down; an encouraging word cheers a person up.

145. To learn, you must love discipline; it is stupid to hate correction.

146. Charm is deceptive, and beauty does not last; but a woman who fears the Lord will be greatly praised.

147. Walk with the wise and become wise; associate with fools and get in trouble.

148. Good people leave an inheritance to their grandchildren, but the sinner's wealth passes to the godly.

149. Those who spare the rod of discipline hate their children. Those who love their children care enough to discipline them.

150. The godly eat to their heart's content, but the belly of the wicked goes hungry.

151. A wise woman builds her home, but a foolish woman tears it down with her own hands.

152. The light of the godly is full of light and joy, but the light of the wicked will be snuffed out.

153. There are six things the Lord hates—no, seven things He detests: haughty eyes, a lying tongue, hands that kill the innocent, a heart that

plots evil, feet that race to do wrong, a false witness who pours out lies, a person who sows discord in a family.

154. But the man who commits adultery is an utter fool, for he destroys himself. He will be wounded and disgraced; his shame will never be erased.

155. Excuses might be found for a thief who steals because he is starving. But if he is caught, he must pay back seven times what he stole—even if he has to sell everything in his house.

156. Don't lust for her beauty; don't let her coy glances seduce you. For a prostitute will bring you to poverty,* but sleeping with another man's wife will cost you your life.
Can a man scoop a flame into his lap and not have his clothes catch on fire?
Can he walk on hot coals and not blister his feet?
So it is with the man who sleeps with another man's wife—who embraces her will not go unpunished.

157. When the storms of life come, the wicked are whirled away, but the godly have a lasting foundation.

158. Hiding hatred makes you a liar; slandering others makes you a fool.

159. Riches won't help on the day of judgment, but right living can save you from death.

160. When the wicked die, their hopes die with them, for they rely on their own feeble strength.

161. Even death and destruction* hold no secrets from the Lord—how much more does He know the human heart?

162. Commit your actions to the Lord, and your plans will succeed.

163. Unfailing love and faithfulness make atonement for sin; by fearing the Lord, people avoid evil.

164. When people's lives please the Lord, even their enemies are at peace with them.

165. The Lord has made everything for His own purposes—even the wicked for a day of disaster.

166. Only simpletons believe everything they're told! The prudent carefully consider their steps.

167. The wise are cautious* and avoid danger; fools plunge ahead with reckless confidence.

168. Evil people will bow before good people; the wicked will bow at the gates of the godly.

169. It is a sin to belittle one's neighbor; blessed are those who help the poor.

170. Fear of the Lord is a life-giving fountain; it offers escape from the snares of death.

171. Rumors are dainty morsels that sink deep into one's heart.

172. Smooth* words may hide a wicked heart, just as a pretty glaze covers a clay pot.

173. Be wise, my child,* and make my heart glad; then I will be able to answer my critics.

174. Never abandon a friend—either yours or your father's. When disaster strikes, you won't have to ask your brother for assistance.

175. A stone is heavy and sand is weighty, but the resentment caused by

a fool is even heavier.

176. As workers who tend a fig tree are allowed to eat the fruit, so workers who protect their employer's interests will be rewarded.

177. A wicked ruler is as dangerous to the poor as a roaring lion or an attacking bear.

178. A hard worker has plenty of food, but a person who chases fantasies ends up in poverty.

179. To reject the law is to praise the wicked; to obey the law is to fight them.

180. An employer who hires a fool or a bystander is like an archer who shoots at random.

181. Don't wait in ambush at the home of the godly, and don't raid the house where the godly live.

182. The wise are mightier than the strong,* and those with knowledge grow stronger and stronger.

183. Like a fluttering sparrow or a darting swallow, an undeserved curse will not land on its intended victim.

184. Don't fret because of evildoers; don't envy the wicked. For evil people have no future; the light of the wicked will be snuffed out.

185. Don't demand an audience with the king or push for a place among the great. It's better to wait for an invitation to the head table than to be sent away in public disgrace.

186. A proverb in the mouth of a fool is as useless as a paralyzed leg.

187. Honoring a fool is as foolish as tying a stone on a slingshot.

188. The mouth of an immoral woman is a dangerous trap; those who

make the Lord angry will fall into it.

189. A youngster's heart is filled with foolishness, but physical discipline will drive it far away.

190. Singing cheerful songs to a person with a heavy heart is like taking someone's coat in cold weather or pouring vinegar in a wound.*

191. Rescue those who are unjustly sentenced to die; save them as they stagger to their death. Don't excuse yourself by saying, "Look, we didn't know," for God understands all hearts, and He sees you.

192. The wicked are punished in place of the godly, and traitors in place of the honest.

193. A secret gift calms anger; a bribe under the table pacifies fury.

194. The Righteous One* knows what is going on in the homes of the wicked; He will bring disaster on them.

195. Evil people desire evil; their neighbors get no mercy from them.

196. Enthusiasm without knowledge is no good; haste makes mistakes.

197. An offended friend is harder to win back than a fortified city. Arguments separate friends like a gate locked with bars.

198. Flipping a coin* can end arguments; it settles disputes between powerful opponents.

199. Giving a gift can open doors; it gives access to important people.

200. Sensible people keep their eyes glued on wisdom, but a fool's eyes wander to the ends of the earth.

201. The wicked take secret bribes to pervert the course of justice.

202. It is painful to be the parent of a fool; there is no joy for the father of a rebel.

203. The crooked heart will not prosper; the lying tongue tumbles into trouble.
204. Anyone who loves to quarrel loves sin; anyone who trusts in high walls invites disaster.
205. Spouting off before listening to the facts is both shameful and foolish.
206. The mouths of fools are their ruin; they trap themselves with their lips.
207. Eloquent words are not fitting for a fool; even less are lies fitting for a ruler.
208. A bribe is like a lucky charm; whoever gives one will prosper.
209. Love prospers when a fault is forgiven, but dwelling on it separates close friends.
210. A single rebuke does more for a person of understanding than a hundred lashes on the back of a fool.
211. It is safer to meet a bear robbed of her cubs than to confront a fool caught in foolishness.
212. With narrowed eyes, people plot evil; with a smirk, they plan their mischief.
213. There is a path before each person that seems right, but it ends in death.
214. From a wise mind comes wise speech; the words of the wise are persuasive.
215. Discretion is a life-giving fountain to those who possess it, but discipline is wasted on fools.

216. A wise servant will rule over the master's disgraceful son and will share the inheritance of the master's children.

217. Pride goes before destruction, and haughtiness before a fall.

218. It's poor judgment to guarantee another person's debt or put up security for a friend.

219. Violent people mislead their companions, leading them down a harmful path.

220. The Lord demands accurate scales and balances; He sets the standards for fairness.

221. A cheerful look brings joy to the heart; good news makes for good health.

222. The heart of the godly thinks carefully before speaking; the mouth of the wicked overflows with evil words.

223. Greed brings grief to the whole family, but those who hate bribes will live.

224. The path of life leads upward for the wise; they leave the grave* behind.

225. If you listen to constructive criticism, you will be at home among the wise.

226. A lazy person's way is blocked with briers, but the path of the upright is an open highway.

227. A bowl of vegetables with someone you love is better than steak with someone you hate.

228. For the despondent, every day brings trouble; for the happy heart, life is a continual feast.

229. The Lord is watching everywhere, keeping His eyes on both the evil and the good.

230. Those who fear the Lord are secure; He will be a refuge for their children.

231. Lazy people don't even cook the game they catch, but the diligent make use of everything they find.

232. It is pleasant to see dreams come true, but fools refuse to turn from evil to attain them.

233. Fools make fun of guilt, but the godly acknowledge it and seek reconciliation.

234. Each heart knows its own bitterness, and no one else can fully share its joy.

235. Laughter can conceal a heavy heart, but when the laughter ends, the grief remains.

236. Thieves are jealous of each other's loot, but the godly are well-rooted and bear their own fruit.

237. Better to be an ordinary person with a servant than to be self-important but have no food.

238. Those who control their tongue will have a long life; opening your mouth can ruin everything.

239. Wise words will win you a good meal, but treacherous people have an appetite for violence.

240. Without wise leadership, a nation falls; there is safety in having many advisers.

241. There's danger in putting up security for a stranger's debt; it's safer not to guarantee another person's debt.

242. The way of the Lord is a stronghold to those with integrity, but it destroys the wicked.

243. The earnings of the godly enhance their lives, but evil people squander their money on sin.

244. My son, obey your father's commands, and don't neglect your mother's instructions. Keep their words always in your heart; tie them around your neck. When you walk, their counsel will lead you; when you sleep, they will protect you.

245. A truthful witness saves lives, but a false witness is a traitor.

246. Let your wife be a fountain of blessing for you. Rejoice in the wife of your youth—she is a loving deer, a graceful doe. Let her breasts satisfy you always; may you always be captivated by her love.

247. Drink water from your own well—share your love only with your wife.*

Why spill the water of your springs in the streets, having sex with just anyone?*

You should reserve it for yourselves; never share it with strangers.

248. For the lips of an immoral woman are as sweet as honey, and her mouth is smoother than oil. But in the end, she is as bitter as poison, as dangerous as a double-edged sword. Her feet go down to death; her steps lead straight to the grave, for she cares nothing about the path of life.

249. Why be captivated, my son, by an immoral woman, or fondle the breast of a promiscuous woman? For the Lord sees clearly what a man does, examining every path he takes. An evil man is held captive by his own sin; they are ropes that catch and hold him. He will die for lack of self-control; he will be lost because of his great foolishness.

250. My child, don't lose sight of common sense and discernment—hang on to them, for they will refresh your soul. They are like jewels on a necklace. They keep you safe on your way, and your feet will not stumble. You can go to bed without fear; you will lie down and sleep soundly. You need not be afraid of sudden disaster or the destruction that comes upon the wicked, for the Lord is your security. He will keep your foot from being caught in a trap.

251. Do not withhold good from those who deserve it, when it's in your power to help them. If you can help your neighbor now, don't say, "Come back tomorrow, and then I'll help you."

252. Don't plot harm against your neighbor, for those who live nearby trust you. Don't pick a fight without reason, when no one has done you harm.

253. Don't be impressed with your own wisdom. Instead, fear the Lord and turn away from evil. Then you will have healing for your body and strength for your bones.

254. Honor the Lord with your wealth and with the best part of everything you produce; then He will fill your barns with grain, and your vats will overflow with good wine.

255. Joyful is the person who finds wisdom, the one who gains understanding. For wisdom is more profitable than silver, and her wages are better than gold. Wisdom is more precious than rubies; nothing you desire can compare with her. She offers you long life in her right hand, and riches and honor in her left.

256. Wisdom is a tree of life to those who embrace her; happy are those who hold her tightly. By wisdom the Lord founded the earth; by understanding He created the heavens. By His knowledge the deep fountains of the earth burst forth, and the dew settles beneath the night sky.

257. She has abandoned her husband and ignores the covenant she made before God. Entering her house leads to death; it is the road to the grave.* The man who visits her is doomed; he will never reach the path of life.

258. Anyone who rebukes a mocker will get an insult in return; anyone who corrects the wicked will get hurt. So don't bother correcting mockers—they will only hate you. But correct the wise, and they will love you. Instruct the wise, and they will be even wiser; teach the righteous, and they will learn even more.

259. Unless the Lord builds a house, the work of the builders is wasted. Unless the Lord protects a city, guarding it with sentries will do no good.

260. The wicked walk into a net; they fall into a pit. A trap grabs them by the heel; a snare holds them tight. A noose lies hidden on the ground; a rope is stretched across their path.

261. Terrors surround the wicked and trouble them at every step. Hunger depletes their strength, and calamity waits for them to stumble. Disease

eats their skin; death devours their limbs. They are torn from the security of their homes and brought down to the king of terrors.

262. The homes of the wicked will burn down; burning sulfur rains on their houses. Their roots will dry up, and their branches will wither. All memory of their existence will fade from the earth; no one will remember their names. They will be thrust from light into darkness, driven from the world.

263. What a holy, awe-inspiring name He has! Fear of the Lord is the foundation of true wisdom. All who obey His commandments will grow in wisdom. Praise Him forever!

264. Light shines in the darkness for the godly. They are generous, compassionate, and righteous. Good comes to those who lend money generously and conduct their business fairly. Such people will not be overcome by evil.

265. Those who are righteous will be long remembered. They do not fear bad news; they confidently trust the Lord to care for them. They are confident and fearless and can face their foes triumphantly. They share freely and give generously to those in need. Their good deeds will be remembered forever; they will have influence and honor. The wicked will see this and be infuriated. They will grind their teeth in anger and slink away, their hopes wasted.

2 | Words of Wisdom

- **WISDOM** - Involves a healthy dose of perspective & the ability to make sound judgements about a matter
- **KNOWLEDGE** - is simply knowing
- **UNDERSTANDING** - ability to comprehend the truths & mysteries of the bible concerning the Gospel of Jesus Christ

All three traits, however, ultimately come from God. As Proverbs 2:6 teaches, "For the Lord gives wisdom; from his mouth comes knowledge and understanding."

1. Holy, Holy, Holy is the Lord God, the Almighty, the One Who always was, Who Is, and Who is still to come.

2. Jesus is the only way to Heaven! Salvation is found in no one else, for there is no other name under heaven given to mankind by which we must be saved.

3. Rest in Me, My child. Give your mind a break from planning and trying to anticipate what will happen. Pray continually, asking My Spirit to take charge of the details of this day. Remember that you are on a journey with Me. When you try to peer into the future and plan for every possibility, you ignore your constant Companion who sustains you moment to moment. As you gaze anxiously into the distance, you don't even feel the strong grip of My hand holding yours. How foolish you are, My child! Remembrance of Me is a daily discipline. Never lose sight of My presence with you. This will keep you resting in Me all day, every day.

4. In the beginning was the "WORD," and the "WORD" was with "GOD," and the "WORD" was "GOD."

5. The Bible don't give life; the Bible leads you to Christ Jesus.

6. Those who worship idols are disgraced— all who brag about their worthless gods.

7. One thing is for certain: the more of ourselves we surrender to God, the more of God we find in ourselves.

8. There is no time man sought out God, but God who sought out man.

9. There is no powerful prayer, but a powerful God who answers prayer.

10. There is no powerful man of God—just a powerful God in man.

11. An empty can makes the loudest noise, so be aware of fools.

12. God does not establish like man does. When He establishes you, there's an outpouring that makes a difference.

13. Jesus is the Prince of Peace! Stop looking for peace in weed, chakras, crystals, sage, meditation, evil eyes, liquor, money, or anything else in this world. You will never find peace.

14. The peace of this world is temporary, but the peace that comes from Jesus is ETERNAL! Those who cling to worthless idols turn away from God's love for them.

15. Never become so thirsty that you drink from every cup presented to you—that's how you get poisoned. Only trust Jesus, because even your earthly mother and father can turn against you.

16. Know that it's not the load that breaks you down, it's the way you carry the load that breaks you.

17. Appreciate those who gossip about you—it's not easy for someone to leave their problems and worry about yours.

18. If everything seems to be under control, you're not going fast enough.

19. Live like you are the poorest, till you can enjoy like the richest.

20. The blessing of the Lord makes a person rich, and He adds no sorrow with it.

21. Remember the former things of old; for I am God, and there is no other; I am God, and there is none like Me, declaring the end from the beginning and from ancient times things not yet done, saying, "My counsel shall stand, and I will accomplish all My purpose," calling a bird of prey from the east, the man of My counsel from a far country. I have spoken, and I will bring it to pass; I have purposed, and I will do it.

22. Joy is actually a command. It comes from obedience. It's cultivated from obedience. Joy is a different dimension, a different realm. It's a spiritual act. Joy is to find the Holy Spirit.

23. The higher you function, the less you impose yourself on others. The more you know, the more you observe. The more love you have to give, the less you offer it up. People have to become receptive to all you are to enjoy what you are.

24. The deeper the love, the more you're misunderstood. The greater your sacrifice, the greater your reward. You must sacrifice being misunderstood to truly function in the fullness of love.

25. How long will you fools hate knowledge? Come and listen to My counsel. I'll share My heart with you and make you wise. I called you so often, but you wouldn't come. I reached out to you, but you paid no attention. You ignored My advice and rejected the correction I offered. So I will laugh when you are in trouble! I will mock you when disaster overtakes you—when calamity overtakes you like a storm, when disaster engulfs you like a cyclone, when anguish and distress overwhelm you. When they cry for help, I will not answer. Though they anxiously search for Me, they will not find Me.

26. What if the Lord had not been on our side when people attacked us? They would have swallowed us alive in their burning anger. The waters would have engulfed us; a torrent would have overwhelmed us. Yes, the raging waters of their fury would have overwhelmed our very lives.

27. Six important guidelines in life: When you are alone, mind your thoughts. When you are with friends, mind your tongue. When you are angry, mind your temper. When you are with a group, mind your behavior. When you are in trouble, mind your emotion. When God starts blessing you, mind your ego.

28. If Satan can talk angels out of heaven, he can talk you into hell. Be mindful of what voices you listen to—the robber can come in all shapes and forms.

29. A relationship with God is not based on what you do; it's based on you accepting what He has made available to you.

30. The concept of prayer laid out by Elohim has never been centered on prayer, but on the grace God has given us that has granted us unlimited access—by Him sacrificing His own Son, our Lord Jesus Christ, on the cross of Calvary. We don't pray to get connected to God; we pray because we are already connected to Him.

31. Ask yourself this simple question: How did you receive salvation, the greatest miracle of them all? Did you fast? Did you spend hours in prayer? Was it not a simple confession of His Lordship over your life? How did He hear you when you cried unto Him while you were still deep in sin on that day of your salvation? Don't you understand that the Lord Jesus is eager to answer you because you have come unto Him, knowing that He has opened the door to salvation by His finished work on the cross? What changed after years of walking with Him? We became foolish by believing in our strength and righteousness because of man's wisdom, and not the wisdom of God.

32. Peace is not found in alcohol or a pill; it's found in the One who died for you—our Lord and Savior Jesus Christ. Let no one fool you. You can have billions in your life, but without Jesus, you will never know real peace.

33. Dear friends, don't be afraid of those who want to kill your body; they cannot do any more to you after that. But I'll tell you whom to fear. Fear God, who has the power to kill you and then throw you into hell. Yes, He's the one to fear. What is the price of five sparrows—two copper coins? Yet God does not forget a single one of them. And the very hairs on your head are all numbered. So don't be afraid; you are more valuable to God than a whole flock of sparrows.

34. Evil people may have piles of money and may store away mounds of clothing, but the righteous will wear that clothing, and the innocent will divide that money. The wicked build houses as fragile as a spider's web, as flimsy as a shelter made of branches. The wicked go to bed rich but wake to find that all their wealth is gone. Terror overwhelms them like a flood. They are blown away in the storms of the night. The east wind carries them away, and they are gone. It sweeps them away. It whirls down on them without mercy. They struggle to flee from its power. But everyone jeers at them and mocks them.

35. Learn to laugh at yourself more freely. Don't take yourself or your circumstances so seriously. Relax and know that I am God with you. When you desire My will above all else, life becomes much less threatening. Stop trying to monitor My responsibilities—things that are beyond your control. Find freedom by accepting the boundaries of your domain. Laughter lightens your load and lifts your heart into heavenly places. Your laughter rises to heaven and blends with angelic melodies of praise. Just as parents delight in the laughter of their children, so I delight in hearing My children laugh. I rejoice when you trust Me enough to enjoy your life lightheartedly. Do not miss the joy of My presence by carrying the weight of the world on your shoulders. Rather, take My yoke upon you and learn from Me. My yoke is comfortable and pleasant; My burden is light and easily borne.

36. I have loved you with an everlasting love. Before time began, I knew you. For years, you swam around in a sea of meaninglessness, searching for love, hoping for hope. All that time, I was pursuing you, aching to embrace you in My compassionate arms. When time was right, I revealed Myself to you, lifted you out of that sea of despair, and set you down on a firm foundation. Sometimes you felt naked, exposed to the revealing

light of My presence. I wrapped an ermine robe around you—My robe of righteousness. I sang you a love song, whose beginning and end are veiled in eternity. I infused meaning into your mind and harmony into your heart. Join Me in singing My song. Together, we will draw others out of darkness into My marvelous light.

37. See your weakness as a reason to pray more. It should not be the reason for sadness or to abandon your post.

38. Soon you will realize God's plan was better all along.

39. When God needs to make a man great, He isolates him. He isolates you to prepare you and exalt you.

40. Satan continues his efforts to make sin less offensive, heaven less appealing, hell less horrific, and the Gospel less urgent.

41. Bad waters doesn't mean evil waters—it means you're simply drinking from wells that God didn't send you to.

42. Be a person who listens, absorbs, and pulls wisdom from the ones whom God has sent.

43. It is the doer of the word that receives things from God. Idle words may entertain men, but they don't reach God.

44. God will not open the door of wisdom to anyone who keeps his Bible shut.

45. For I am not ashamed of the gospel, for it is the power of God for salvation to everyone who believes.

46. The more you dwell in the secret place of prayer, the more of God's light you will attract.

47. No matter how unsteady the world appears to be, I will continue to live steady, talk steady, shout steady.

48. *Your vision needs to come to an end for God's vision to begin.*

49. *Many people don't realize that the idol they've replaced God with in their lives is their emotion.*

50. *Dismantle your fears and apprehensions and come and sit with Me in the quiet of the evening. Sit with Me in calmness and stillness and allow Me to guide you into the unknown realms you have not yet explored nor encountered. Allow Me to speak with whispers. Allow the subtlety and nuance of My engagement with your heart to inspire you as I feed you from the wealth of delicacies from My table. In Me you will find all manner of delights, adventure, and treasure, and in Me you will encounter truth and adjustment. In Me you will experience peace and joy—and will do so without stress, expense, or striving. So dismantle the busyness of your heart and mind and allow My Spirit to slowly and gently engage with you. As you do, you will come to see we are one, bonded together, having nothing separating us whatsoever.*

51. *Demons detest praise, but also it invites the presence of the Lord, and God inhabits the praises of His people. For the Lord taketh pleasure in His people: He will beautify the meek with salvation. Let the saints be joyful in glory; let them sing aloud on their beds. Let the high praises of God be in their mouth, and a two-edged sword in their hand. Praise did not get Paul and Silas out of prison, but it got God in with them! Praise loosed the shackles and kicked down the doors of the prison, and it does the same for those in demonic bondage—it brings God into the situation. The blood will torment demons, but they do not have to obey the blood. The blood is for protection, cleansing, forgiveness, and healing. The holy, unblemished, spotless blood of the Lord Jesus will torment demon powers; however, it is the commands in the name of Jesus Christ that they must obey.*

52. *Yes, Jesus hung out with prostitutes and drunkards and outcasts. Here's the thing though—by the time Jesus was finished with these people, they weren't prostitutes or drunkards or outcasts anymore. Jesus came to transform people, not indulge them. Christianity is about surrender, not comfort. We are to align ourselves to His standard, not the other way around.*

53. Demons cannot stand praise music, as I just mentioned. They are not only annoyed by it, but also tormented by it. You see, that used to be their job—they were once the angels of praise whose appointment was to sing and praise the Lord. It is a constant reminder that they made a fatal mistake in following Lucifer in rebellion. My experience is that you can praise your way through anything and everything! Not only do demons detest praise, but also it invites the presence of the Lord, and He inhabits the praises of His people.

54. Give up the illusion that you deserve a problem-free life. Part of you is still hungering for the resolution of all difficulties—this is a false hope! As I told My disciples, "In the world you will have trouble." Link your hope not to problem-solving in this life, but to the promise of an eternity of problem-free life in heaven. Instead of seeking perfection in this fallen world, pour your energy into seeking Me—the Perfect One. It is possible to enjoy Me and glorify Me in the midst of adverse circumstances. In fact, My Light shines most brightly through believers who trust Me in the dark. That kind of trust is supernatural—a production of My indwelling Spirit. When things seem all wrong, trust Me anyway. I am much less interested in right circumstances than in right responses to whatever comes your way. "I have told you these things, so that in Me you may have peace. In this world you will have trouble. But take heart! I have overcome the world."

55. "Don't let your hearts be troubled. Trust in God, and trust also in Me. There is more than enough room in My Father's home. If this were not so, would I have told you that I am going to prepare a place for you? When everything is ready, I will come and get you, so that you will always be with Me where I am." Jesus told them, "I AM THE WAY, THE TRUTH, AND THE LIFE. NO ONE CAN COME TO THE FATHER EXCEPT THROUGH ME."

56. When the enemy wants you to waste time, he gives you a wrong purpose that God never intended for you.

57. If Daniel can trust God in the lion's den, you can trust God in your stresses and worries.

58. The outcome of believing in God's word: "You possess the things that His Word has guaranteed."

59. Remember, as a child of God, whatever situation we find ourselves in—God wouldn't have allowed it unless He had a purpose.

~Don't just go through it. Grow through it~

60. Jealousy can hide in compliments, envy can hide in support, but hate cannot hide in love.

61. Not once in the Bible does it say "worry about it," "stress over it," or "figure it out," but over and over it clearly says trust God.

62. Move accordingly to God's leadership, not your emotions—that will only lead you astray.

63. No matter what you are going through as a Christian, stay true to Jesus Christ. Do not despair. Do not give up. Do not look down. (Pray, worship, give God praise, glorify Jesus' name, walk in authority, dance, smile, believe, never lose faith.) (In Truth and in Spirit)
Soon you'll have your testimony.
Soon you will testify.

64. Don't let your situation mislead you and cause you to start doubting your God. A man may be poor and yet be a friend of God. You can be sick in body and yet be one of God's favorites—even a candidate for heaven.

65. Jesus Christ came to pay a debt He didn't owe, because we owed a debt we couldn't pay.

66. You cannot drink from the cup of the Lord and from the cup of demons too. You cannot eat at the Lord's table, and eat at the table of demons too.

67. When you experience problems, you may not want to be in that problem—but God does—so that He can reveal His power to man in that problem.

68. Spiritual growth is knowing "To live is for Christ; to lay to rest is to gain." Whether we live or rest, we belong to Jesus Christ.

69. In life, understand that those whom you help will most likely be the ones who seek to destroy you. In all things, do not get tired of doing good—do it for the sake of God.

70. Stop being a fan of a celebrity who doesn't even know you. Be a fan of Jesus Christ, who died for you.

71. But God's truth stands firm like a foundation stone with this inscription: "The Lord knows those who are His," and "All who belong to the Lord must turn away from evil."

72. People remember the experience you give them. So no matter the outcome, always end things in peace. You don't want to burn a bridge with people you just might need again.

73. They may take away everything from you, but if they haven't taken your ability to pray, then they have done nothing—because with prayer, you will always experience triumph.

74. Since you have been raised to new life with Christ, set your sights on the realities of heaven, where Christ sits in the place of honor at God's right hand. Think about the things of heaven, not the things of earth, for you died to this life, and your real life is hidden with Christ in God. And when Christ, who is your life, is revealed to the whole world, you will share in all His glory.

75. Be vigilant of all who are in your surroundings. Pay close attention. Their actions, their reactions—that is all you need to know if they belong or need to be cut off completely. Don't ever second-guess, even with family. Family can be number one wishing on your downfall.

76. When the enemy plans to attack you, and you are a blessing even in the process, the Spirit of God will put confusion in their midst.

77. A person is made right with God by faith in Jesus Christ, not by obeying the law. So believing in Christ Jesus makes you right with God—not because anyone has obeyed the law, for no one will ever be made right with God by the law.

78. Stop praying for temporary things. When God blesses you, a generation is secured. Your children—and your children's children—will all be under the same covering.

79. God said, "He will never fail us." God said, "He will never abandon us." So we can say with confidence, "The Lord is our helper, so we will have no fear; what can mere people do to us?"

80. Don't confuse increase for the blessing. When the blessings come, it doesn't just increase finances—it increases every area of your life: your relationships, your business, everything to do with you will prosper. They will all be the evidence of the blessing.

81. God's blessings increase everything. That's why when the blessings come, there is no more room for sorrow—because where will sorrow go? The blessings fill everything, so you don't have room to receive sorrow.

82. "If you want to boast, boast only about the Lord." When people commend themselves, it doesn't count for much. The important thing is for the Lord to commend them.

83. Learn that when you talk too much, you become a dangerous person. Learn that when you are a person who talks too much, God is not there. If there's one thing we need to know, it's how to control our mouths.

84. Reposition yourself for endurance. The Holy Spirit always brings us to a place of decision, but He will not make that decision for us. Look at our Lord and Savior Jesus Christ: the night before He was crucified, He had to make a decision—and He prayed to His Father. But many of us today just want to do our own will and don't bother about God's will. Brethren, this is a dangerous mission.

85. Church is my college.
Heaven is my university.
Jesus is my principal.
The Holy Spirit is my teacher.
Angels are my classmates.
The Bible is my study book.
Trials and temptations are my exams.
Winning souls are my assignments.
Prayer is my attendance.
Crown of life is my degree.
Praise and worship is my motto.
Enroll today—there is room for all, and tuition is free.

86. Our qualification comes from God. He has enabled us to be ministers of His new covenant. This is a covenant not of written laws, but of the Spirit. The old written covenant ends in death, but under the new covenant, the Spirit gives life.

87. We as God's children should try to please everyone in everything we do. We should not just do what is best for ourselves—we should do what is best for others, so that many may be saved. We should imitate Christ Jesus in all we do.

88. God chose me; I did not choose God. I believe in God not because my parents told me to, or because my church told me to, but because I've experienced His presence and power in my life—and how awesome He is.

89. As a child of God, know this: demons see, but they don't monitor. When they see something they find interesting, they can use humans to pursue it, but they are not idols watching your life. It doesn't work like that. The real concern is with humans—because they are the ones who monitor and can be influenced by evil. A devil watching us doesn't mean much. But a person who is used by the devil can be very dangerous. It's the actions of people influenced by evil that cause disruption and destruction—not the devil on his own.

90. For the grace of God has been revealed, bringing salvation to all people. And we are instructed to turn from godless living and sinful

pleasures. We should live in this evil world with wisdom, righteousness, and devotion to God—while we look forward with hope to that wonderful day when the glory of our great God and Savior, Jesus Christ, will be revealed.

91. For a time is coming when people will no longer listen to sound and wholesome teaching. They will follow their own desires and will look for teachers who will tell them whatever their itching ears want to hear. They will reject the truth and chase after myths. But you should keep a clear mind in every situation. Don't be afraid of suffering for the Lord. Work at telling others the Good News.

92. For at just the right time, Christ will be revealed from heaven by the blessed and only Almighty God—the King of all kings and Lord of all lords. He alone can never die, and He lives in light so brilliant that no human can approach Him. No human eye has ever seen Him, nor ever will. All honor and power to Him forever! Amen.

93. Lord, I submit to Your will even when it hurts. I'll still trust You even through the pain. Thank You that You have not looked upon my flaws or mistakes like man does. Sometimes I don't understand how You could choose a very imperfect person like me. Without Your grace, I am nothing. Through all of this, Lord, I choose Your grace.

94. Now the Holy Spirit tells us clearly that in the last times some will turn away from the true faith. They will follow deceptive spirits and teachings that come from demons. These people are hypocrites and liars, and their consciences are dead. They will say it is wrong to be married and wrong to eat certain foods—but God created those foods to be eaten with thanks by faithful people who know the truth. Since everything God created is good, we should not reject any of it but receive it with thanks. For we know it is made acceptable by the Word of God and prayer.

95. The cure for the flesh is death; the cure for the soul is the Word of God; the cure for the spirit is intimacy with God.

96. Faith is the ability to see God's strength in capacity—to know that the God who created the heavens and the earth has the power to heal you, deliver you, prosper you, and set you free. He will take care of you. God, the Giver of life, has the ability to do anything for you. Faith should be in God's capacity, not in the things that we want or hope for.

97. God will provide rest for you who are being persecuted, and also for us, when the Lord Jesus appears from heaven. He will come with His mighty angels in flaming fire, bringing judgment on those who don't know God and on those who refuse to obey the Good News of our Lord Jesus. They will be punished with eternal destruction, forever separated from the Lord and from His glorious power. When He comes on that day, He will receive glory from His holy people—praise from all who believe. And this includes you, for you believed what we told you about Him.

98. Through our endurance and faithfulness in all the persecutions and hardships we are suffering, God will use this persecution to show His justice and to make you worthy of His Kingdom, for which you are suffering. In His justice, He will pay back those who persecute you.

99. Brothers and sisters, we urge you to warn those who are lazy, encourage those who are timid, take tender care of those who are weak, be patient with everyone. See that no one pays back evil for evil, but always try to do good to each other and to all people.

100. Always be joyful. Never stop praying. Be thankful in all circumstances, for this is God's will for you who belong to Christ Jesus. Do not stifle the Holy Spirit. Do not scoff at prophecies, but test everything that is said. Hold on to what is good. Stay away from every kind of evil.

101. It's okay to pray for directions, but there is a place you get to where you act with God—where God can reason with you. Not because God needs your opinion, but because you have matured enough that God will not even do anything without sitting with you and saying, "This is what I'm trying to do. What do you think?" That is the place of spiritual maturity that we believers should reach.

102. Have you never heard? Have you never understood? The Lord is the everlasting God, the Creator of all the earth. He never grows weak or weary. No one can measure the depths of His understanding. He

gives power to the weak and strength to the powerless. Even youths will become weak and tired, and young men will fall in exhaustion. But those who trust in the Lord will find new strength. They will soar high on wings like eagles. They will run and not grow weary. They will walk and not faint.

103. Let there be no sexual immorality, impurity, or greed among you. Such sins have no place among God's people. Obscene stories, foolish talk, and coarse jokes—these are not for you. Instead, let there be thankfulness to God. You can be sure that no immoral, impure, or greedy person will inherit the Kingdom of Christ and of God. For a greedy person is an idolater, worshiping the things of this world.

104. Living in the light—imitate God, therefore, in everything you do, because you are His dear children. Live a life filled with love, following the example of Christ Jesus. He loved us and offered Himself as a sacrifice for us, a pleasing aroma to God.

105. When God gives you skill, if you do not practice, then you won't gain experience. If you practice and you fail in the practice, it is not a failure—it's a lesson. It's still experience. The problem is people are so afraid to fail that they don't get experience, and experience is the only thing that actually sharpens your skills. So when God gives you skill, He gives it spiritually, but you must grow in it physically.

106. Don't be misled—you cannot mock the justice of God. You will always harvest what you plant. Those who live only to satisfy their own sinful nature will harvest decay and death from that sinful nature. But those who live to please the Spirit will harvest everlasting life from the Spirit. So let's not get tired of doing what is good. At just the right time, we will reap a harvest of blessing if we don't give up.

107. The situations and challenges you are going through as a child of God do not matter to Jesus Christ. What matters to Jesus Christ is how you handle them—because how you handle them determines your future.

108. Do you think that Joseph would have made it to the throne if he had harbored bitterness in his heart about the unfair treatment he

received at the hands of his brothers—and then again at the hands of Pharaoh, who put him in prison although he was innocent?

109. There is no mountain that God cannot level, no barriers or blockades that can stop God's momentum in our lives. Because of Jesus Christ, there is no valley or ditch that won't be filled, no demonic onslaught that won't end with our victory. We are more than conquerors. Jesus Christ did say, "It is finished," on the cross of Calvary—so it is so.

110. If My people, which are called by My name, shall humble themselves and pray, and seek My face, and turn from their wicked ways; then will I hear from heaven, and will forgive their sin, and will heal their land.

111. It is in the mind of God to answer prayers—even when He seems not to respond immediately to our petitions. So, if you are following the right process and seem not to be getting results, don't get discouraged. God is preparing you for something greater than what you want. All you need to do is be patient and wait upon the Lord, who will not leave you without a solution. Those that laugh at you for your patience will testify about your result.

112. Today, everyone wants to be great—but not everyone wants to go through God's process. God's process matters; it will help you maintain the result you get from Him. If the process you go through is not in line with the ways of God, the result will not stand the test of time. If you ignore the process and focus only on the result, you may likely not have the patience to differentiate between God's supply and Satan's bait. To become God's person, you must follow His process. God wants us to prosper in all areas—He does not want us to succeed only financially while losing ourselves to conditions.

113. Proof Jesus is real: because this whole world only mocks Christianity. No other religion is hated the way Christianity is. Why? Because their spirits and demons know the name of the Lord Jesus Christ—and they fear it.

114. As a child of God, you can boldly say that the Word of God is a lamp for your feet and a light to your path. The Word is the only way you can live a successful life, a joyful life, because it gives you insight and direction. You cannot walk in the dark.

115. Nobody has any excuse for remaining the way they are. There is always a way out—Jesus Christ is the way. If you want to be dignified, honored, respected, and privileged, you must learn to be humble. Because those that Christ intends to honor, He humbles—to make them feel their own unworthiness.

116. Your place of destiny requires you to be strong-hearted. Take note that God is always on time. He is never too late and never too early. He is building character and rightful focus in you—to mature you and prepare you to maintain your blessing when it comes. When you know the purpose of your situation, whatever happens midway will not dictate your direction, since it is meant to strengthen you. As a believer, your situation calls for thanksgiving. Praising God should be your attitude toward trials, because when trials come, your promotion is near. We urge you today to pick yourself up and repair your relationship with Jesus Christ.

117. Stop deceiving yourselves. If you think you are wise by this world's standards, you need to become a fool to be truly wise. For the wisdom of this world is foolishness to God. As the Scriptures say, "He traps the wise in the snare of their own cleverness." And again, "The Lord knows the thoughts of the wise; He knows they are worthless." So don't boast about yourself or about following a particular human leader.

118. Jesus Christ is the same yesterday, today, and forever. This means that whatever is rooted in the Lord Jesus is permanent, stable, incontestable, and untouchable. Life is all about taking tough decisions. For example, when people insult you, you can either ignore the insult in the spirit of forgiveness, or retaliate in any manner you may choose. When you are in need of help, you can decide to run to God or run to your worldly friends. The issue is whether you are making the right decision. Unless the decisions we make are rooted in God's Word, they will not stand at the time of great need.

119. What I am saying, dear brothers and sisters, is that our physical bodies cannot inherit the Kingdom of God. These dying bodies cannot inherit what will last forever. But let me reveal to you a wonderful secret: we will not all die, but we will all be transformed! It will happen in a

moment, in the blink of an eye, when the last trumpet is blown. For when the trumpet sounds, those who have died will be raised to live forever. And we who are living will also be transformed. For our dying bodies must be transformed into bodies that will never die; our mortal bodies must be transformed into immortal bodies.

120. The power of speaking in tongues—if you have the ability to speak in tongues, you will be talking only to God, since people won't be able to understand you. You will be speaking by the power of the Spirit—but it will all be mysterious.

121. If gold must be gold, it must pass through fire. Anytime you are face to face with uncommon challenges, do not lose heart—they may be to prepare you for the uncommon blessings that are waiting ahead of you. Because uncommon blessings always attract uncommon challenges. When you know this as a child of God, your confession will always be, "Whether You save me or not, I will continue to serve You, because I know You are my Savior! I know You are God all the time."

122. A spiritual gift is given to each of us so we can help each other. To one person, the Spirit gives the ability to give wise advice; to another, the same Spirit gives a message of special knowledge. The same Spirit gives great faith to another, and to someone else, the Spirit gives the gift of healing. He gives one person the power to perform miracles, and another the ability to prophesy. He gives someone else the ability to discern whether a message is from the Spirit of God or from another spirit. Still another person is given the ability to speak unknown languages, while another is given the ability to interpret what is being said. It is the one and only Spirit who distributes all these gifts. He alone decides which gift each person should have.

123. You should recognize that what I am saying is a command from the Lord Himself. But if you do not recognize this, you yourself will not be recognized. So, my dear brothers and sisters, be eager to prophesy, and don't forbid speaking in tongues—but be sure that everything is done properly and in order.

124. You will win this fight—but you have to press harder than you've

pressed before. The enemy has tried to get you to give up and quit. The enemy has caused you to shrink back from the fight because you're so close to the brink of supernatural victory and overwhelming success that he is scared. He's tried every little last thing. But if you will just press a little harder, if you will push a little longer, if you will turn off the TV and put down your phone and pick up your sword—you will deal the victory blow swiftly. Refocus yourself, rise and fight again. The victory is yours.

125. Remember this today: Jesus died so you can live. He was crucified so He can live in and through you—to bring more lost souls into His Kingdom. Remember what Paul said to the Galatian church: he had the revelation that he was crucified with Christ and that his life was no longer his own. He understood that Christ lived in him and that he lived his life by faith in the Son of God who loved him, died for him, and rose again for him. Have the same mind and walk in this truth.

126. If there's a Goliath in front of you, that means there's a David inside of you. And if Goliath is always there, that means most definitely you are chosen by God—so walk in your calling. Remember also that the chosen get attacked more by the enemy. Why, you may ask? Because you are representing danger for their kingdom. You will forever be a target. So don't be afraid—no one can remove what's for God in God's hand.

127. Prayer is not the art of begging or the expression of desperation to the Lord. Prayer is an act of faith—understanding that the Lord Jesus has the power to change any situation. Where there is no faith, there is no prayer at all. No matter how many hours or days you put in, it's a waste of time. God does not listen to words—He listens to the faith. Where there is faith, there is rest. Where there is faith, there are praises. Where there is faith, there is a divine assurance beyond understanding that it is well. Faith is the only language that pleases the Lord God Jehovah—not much speaking.

128. Silence is the absence of sound, but it's also a dimension in the spirit where one receives revelation from the throne room. Learning how to remain quiet in soul and calm in spirit, in order to discern what is happening in the spirit world and see what the Lord is saying, is vital to navigating seer dimensions.

129. The fall of man came because someone poisoned man against God and His intentions for man. The most dangerous demonic weapon is confusion; confusion is worse than witchcraft.

130. A sign to know that you're chosen is that you start to carry burdens that are not yours.

131. There's a process that God has to put you through in order for you to display everything God has put in you.

132. You can choose your right perspective. Your life experience has caused your natural mind to have one perspective, but you have the mind of Christ and the Word of God. They offer you a different perspective on the issues of life. The enemy will try to sell you his perspective on events that unfold in your life. Don't buy into his evil visions—choose instead, by God's will, to look at life through the lens of the Word and through the eyes of eternity. You'll be more joyful, wiser, stronger, and more powerful.

133. When people let you down, break their word to you, or do something you've asked them over and over again not to do—don't take it personally. When you take it as a personal jab, your heart is more likely to become disappointed, offended, or resentful. Many people are thinking about themselves—what they need the most and how to get it. Don't take their actions personally.

134. Choosing to align your heart with My heart at the beginning of each day is one of the wisest decisions you can make. When you awake, the enemy does not slumber, and he wastes no time in chattering to your soul about the cares of your life—often before you get out of bed in the morning. Align your heart and mind with My heart and mind each morning. Cast your cares on Christ as they arise, and know that your every need is covered. If I wouldn't think it, don't allow yourself to think it.

135. Don't say about yourself the negative things people say about you. What do they know? Say about yourself what I say about you. I am your Creator; I know you intimately. The power of life and death is in

your tongue. Don't think about what they're thinking about you—think about what I'm thinking about you. What I think about you is all that matters, and I'm thinking good thoughts toward you. I've got great and mighty exploits for you to do. What I think and say about you is in My Word and in My heart. Don't listen to the critics—listen to Me.

136. My light is greater than deep darkness, than gross darkness, than the darkest of dark. My light will overcome any and every measure of darkness clouding your mind, your body, and your family. Let My light shine from within you, and you will blind the enemies of light. My light will illuminate your path and expose the enemy's darkness that aims to trip you up and slip you up. Jesus is the Light of the world. Now, it's your turn—burn and shine, and the enemy will flee.

137. You can do anything you set your mind to, but you will be better off if you do what I've set My mind for you to do. Don't follow your own wisdom; it will take you only so far. Man's wisdom apart from Me is often flawed. Depend on My wisdom, and you will walk in peaceful paths. Set your heart to follow My heart. I know the mind of the Father—He loves you and has a good plan for you. So be determined, but determine to do the Father's will rather than your own, and you will always be pleased with the outcome.

138. When you choose to live in love, you choose to live in God—and God in you! What a wonderful blessing: "And we have known and believed the love that God has for us. God is love, and he who abides in love abides in God, and God in him."

139. The enemy is trying to move us off the position of faith. Stand firm. Stand strong knowing that whatever can be shaken will be shaken, but you shall not be moved when you trust in Me. I've got you in My hands, and I'm able to make you stand in the evil day. I'm able to make you stand in the midst of the battle. I'm able to make you stand when all hell is breaking loose against you. I am able to make you stand. Don't bow down to the imaginations in your mind—bow down to Me. Don't bow to the spirit of fear. Don't bow to that spirit of discouragement. Bow to Me.

140. For those who are seated on the highway of life—worrying about tomorrow, despairing about life's uncertainties, and murmuring about life's problems—there is good news for you. We serve a God who oftentimes brings good out of evil. He uses unpleasant circumstances to uncover His mighty grace and promise in the lives of His people. Joseph was a man who faced rejection from his own people, but God used his rejection for his advancement. What is your situation? Are you rejected, disappointed, or abandoned? Are you in pain and don't know what life will bring? Leave it for God. Nobody can replace God's plan for your life.

141. When we go through temptation, we fail to realize that most of the time, God is helping us to build character so that when we get to the place of our destiny, we will not crack, explode, and lose it all. God has purposefully kept us in the dark concerning future events so we can always be alert, watchful, and prayerful. 1 Corinthians 1:27 teaches us that God sometimes works most wisely and most powerfully in a way directly opposite to human expectations. Do not allow your situation to weigh you down. A real Christian depends upon God's grace, puts his trust in Christ alone. It is this grace that gives us hope that no matter the situation, the best is yet to come.

142. The Son is the image of the invisible God, the firstborn over all creation. For in Him all things were created: things in heaven and on earth, visible and invisible, whether thrones or powers or rulers or authorities. All things have been created through Him and for Him. He is before all things, and in Him all things hold together. And He is the head of the body, the church; He is the beginning and the firstborn from among the dead, so that in everything He might have the supremacy. For God was pleased to have all His fullness dwell in Him, and through Him to reconcile to Himself all things.

143. As long as the earth remains, there will be seedtime and harvesttime. If you want a harvest, you must sow a seed. If you want a generous harvest, you must sow a generous seed. For he who sows sparingly reaps sparingly, but he who sows generously reaps generously. But watch your seed—water it with the word of your mouth. Don't curse your seed in the ground. Don't let the enemy choke the seed with faithless words from your heart. Believe Me for the harvest.

144. Walk in love and keep healthy boundaries while you walk—these two things do not contradict each other; no, they work together. You need to walk in love with yourself, and if your boundaries are so low that you are worn out, then you won't love others well. Walk in love, but keep healthy boundaries.

145. Our relationship with God should be our number one focus, because we know that if we take care of that first, we have nothing else to worry about. God will take care of everything else, and everything will be in order. That's when you will encounter real "rest"—meaning you rest in the Lord, knowing no other rest can compare. That leads to real joy, a sound mind, no confusion; you will know what real peace is, and you will never want to leave that resting place.

146. That anxiety doesn't stand a chance against God's peace. Peace is your promised portion through the blood of Christ.

147. Guard your heart in this season from the serpent's seduction to lure you to sleep. Guard the anointing that has been entrusted to you from the kingdom to contend for the supernatural in this generation. Guard your space in the secret place, for the lure of the world can cause you to be careless with the anointing upon you. We are in a season that we must be vigilant and alert for us to release the prophetic decree. Again I say, guard the anointing!

148. Not everyone who calls out to Me 'Jesus', 'Lord! Lord!' will enter the kingdom of heaven—only those who actually do the will of My Father in heaven will enter. On judgment day many will say to Me, 'Lord! Lord! We prophesied in Your name and cast out demons in Your name and performed many miracles in Your name.' But I will reply, 'I never knew you. Get away from Me, you who break God's laws.' Anyone who listens to My teaching and follows it is wise, like a person who builds a house on solid rock.

149. God wants to move in your life, but some people need to be moved out. Hear Me: the wrong people—even in the right season—will create nothing but confusion for you. Change will come to your life by changing the people around you. I will give you a new song and place before you a door with a new path in life. A door of abundance will stand before you, and you will shut out the past for good. Your access code to greatness will no longer be hacked by the enemy. Your greatest blessing awaits your greatest surrender to Me.

150. Hope is found in the name of Jesus. God will always do something greater within you than you ever expected. When we place our faith in Jesus Christ, what was broken is made whole. The key is running towards the power of Jesus and giving Him your brokenness. He wants your heart, your mind, and your strength. He wants all of you! Today, let us choose to run after our Savior so that He can take our brokenness and make us whole.

151. The truth is, the heart of a man is what the Lord looks at. God is the only one who truly knows us 100%. This is why we should put our trust fully in the Lord Jesus—because He knows what is best for us. By doing this, He will reward us greatly. "I the Lord search the heart and test the mind, to give every man according to his ways, according to the fruit of his deeds."

152. Greatest man in history: had no servants, yet they called Him Master; had no degree, yet they called Him Teacher; had no medicines, yet they called Him Healer. He had no army, yet kings feared Him. He won no military battles, yet He conquered the world. He committed no crime, yet they crucified Him. He was buried in a tomb, yet He lives today. His name is Jesus, the Son of God—our Lord.

153. Jesus is the stronger man. Jesus rightly described your enemy as a strongman—but Jesus is the Stronger Man. Jesus is greater than any enemy stronghold and can deliver you from evil. Cry out to Me in His name, and you will meet face to face with your Deliverer. Jesus will empower you to overcome the strongman who has kept you in bondage. By way of the resurrection life and power that dwells inside of you, He will empower you to break free from every tie that binds you to death. The strongman may have you bound, but the Stronger Man in you will lead you into liberty.

154. What worries you doesn't frustrate Me. What keeps you up at night

doesn't keep Me up at night. What scares you and steals your peace does not move Me. Do you want to know why? Because I am not giving ear to the voice of the enemy. I hear his chatter against your mind, but it does not move Me. I see your end from your beginning. I created you in My image. I am standing with you, living inside of you, and leading and guiding you. Stop allowing the enemy to worry you, keep you up at night, scare you, and steal your peace. Walk with Me.

155. God is saying to you: stop worrying about it. I made a way for you last time, and I will make a way this time too. Get up and start your day. Whatever you are worrying about, I have a plan. I'm bigger than your fear. I'm with you. I'm stronger than the obstacle in front of you. I won't leave you. Have faith, My child.

156. Before you can go in the strength you have, you have to stop worshiping your weaknesses. You have spent enough time in your life, in the form of the excuses you made, worshiping your weakness. For every time you make an excuse about something God called you to do, you worship the weakness instead of worshiping the God who gives you strength.

157. "Number one killer of clarity is disobedience." "There is no new beginning outside of clarity." "When your gift satisfies a need, then there is a calling." "God will cause men not to see us because He is developing us." "It is light to God, but confusing to men."

158. "God alone understands the way to wisdom; He knows where it can be found. For He looks throughout the whole earth and sees everything under the heavens. He decided how hard the winds should blow and how much rain should fall. He made the laws for the rain and laid out a path for the lightning. Then He saw wisdom and evaluated it. He set it in place and examined it thoroughly, and this is what He says to all humanity: 'The fear of the Lord is true wisdom; to forsake evil is real understanding.'"

159. Sex won't satisfy you. Fame won't satisfy you. Drugs won't satisfy you. Money won't satisfy you. Alcohol won't satisfy you. Many degrees won't satisfy you. All your success won't satisfy you. Life is empty without Jesus. He is the only one who can satisfy your heart.

160. Speak these words to your spirit daily: I am forgiven of all sins. I am healed of all diseases. I am living a redeemed life. I am sanctified by truth. I am God's beloved child. I am perfected by love. I am full of joy. I have no need. I am bought by Your blood, Lord Jesus. I belong to You, not myself. I am Your vessel, Most High God. I am loved by Jesus. I am loved by my Father God. I am loved by the Holy Spirit. I have a future and hope in You. I will fulfill my destiny. I hear my Good Shepherd's voice. I do not follow a stranger's voice. I am surrounded by Your love. I walk by faith, not by sight. I am the righteousness of Christ. I owe no one anything but to love them. I love my brothers and sisters in Christ. I walk in righteousness, peace, and joy. I am surrounded by favor.

161. But do people know where to find wisdom? Where can they find understanding? No one knows where to find it, for it is not found among the living. "It is not here," says the ocean. "Nor is it here," says the sea. It cannot be bought with gold; it cannot be purchased with silver. It's worth more than all the gold of Ophir, greater than precious onyx or lapis lazuli. Wisdom is more valuable than gold and crystal. It cannot be purchased with jewels mounted in fine gold. Coral and jasper are worthless in trying to get it. The price of wisdom is far above rubies. Precious peridot from Ethiopia cannot be exchanged for it. It's worth more than the purest gold. But do people know where to find wisdom? Where can they find understanding? It is hidden from the eyes of all humanity—even the sharp-eyed birds in the sky cannot discover it. Destruction and death say, "We've heard only rumors of where wisdom can be found." God alone understands the way to wisdom; He knows where it can be found.

162. Seek to live in My love, which covers a multitude of sins—both yours and others'. Wear My love like a cloak of light, covering you from head to toe. Have no fear, for perfect love decimates fear. Look at other people through lenses of love; see them from My perspective. This is how you walk in the light, and it pleases Me. I want My body of believers to be radiant with the light of My presence. How I grieve when pockets of darkness increasingly dim the love-light. Return to Me, your first love! Gaze at Me in the splendor of holiness, and My love will once again envelop you in light.

163. *I want you to be all Mine, filled with the light of My presence. I gave everything for you by living as a man, then dying for your sins and living again. Hold back nothing from Me. Bring your most secret thoughts into the light of My love. Anything you bring to Me I transform and cleanse from darkness. I know everything about you—far more than you know of yourself—but I restrain My yearning to "fix" you, waiting instead for you to come to Me for help. Imagine the divine restraint this requires—for I have all power in heaven and on earth. Seek My face with a teachable spirit. Come into My presence with thanksgiving, desiring to be transformed.*

164. *Press in to see. Don't allow the enemy to cause you to see through a glass darkly those things I'm trying to show you plainly. Determine to come up higher through the persistence of your will to study My Word and press into My presence. Don't be satisfied with seeing through the glass darkly. Don't be satisfied with knowing in part and seeing in part and moving in part when I am speaking expressly to your heart. Press in for the part that you have not seen—the part the enemy does not want you to see. Press in, press in, press in. Press in, press in.*

3 | PRAYERS (Part I)

**JESUS ANSWERED,
"I AM THE WAY, AND THE TRUTH, AND THE LIFE,
NO ONE COMES TO THE FATHER EXCEPT THROUGH ME."
-JOHN 14:6**

Blessings, Children of the Most High God—Jehovah God.
Now, after reading, meditating, and living as an example of what you've read in Proverbs—the Word of knowledge, wisdom, and understanding—making God's words a part of your everyday life, in faith I know so much has changed in your life. Because it happened for me, I'm testifying that it changed my life so much. To God all the glory belongs.

So, Father God, we give You all the glory for beginning to change our lives for the better. But we believe the best is yet to come. In Jesus Christ's powerful name, Amen.

Having it all and not having Jesus Christ as your Lord and Savior, not having your name written in the Book of Life—I can assure you, you have nothing.
Yes, you have nothing. All will come to pass, but Jesus is eternal. When you drink the Living Water, you shall never thirst again.

John 3:16 - For God so loved the world that He gave His one and only Son, that whoever believes in Him shall not perish but have eternal life.

The Moment of Truth.

The moment of reality. A day, a time, a date to remember that will mark your life forever, that will change your life forever. A moment where you can choose Jesus, giving your life to Jesus Christ as Lord and Savior forever—your Redeemer, Protector, Healer, Deliverer, your safe refuge.

Wanna Give Your Life to Jesus?

Lift up your right hand. Close your eyes and say this prayer—with conviction, with truth, with all that's within you:

Lord Jesus, today in this place, I declare my love for You.
Today in this place, I declare that You are the Son of the Living God.
I receive You as my Savior, as my Lord, and as my King.
Truthfully and genuinely, I declare that I am a recipient of eternal life.
I also declare that the power of sin, Satan, hell, and the grave is broken over my life. From today and forever, I am a child of God, washed by the blood of the Lamb. I go forward ever, and backward never.
In Jesus' mighty name I pray, Amen.

Congratulations!

The Right Channel to Pray

Lord, I'm a sinner. I don't deserve to be in Your presence. I'm the worst sinner on this earth. If You look around the whole world, I'm the worst sinner. Show me Your mercy, please. I have no justification at all. I'm the worst sinner—show me Your mercy, show me Your mercy.

Whatever sin I might have committed—knowingly or unknowingly—whether through action, unforgiveness in my heart, lying, stealing, killing, destruction, fornication, watching pornography, or masturbating—whatever sin I might have committed, wash me with Your precious blood. Cleanse me, Lord. I'm in Your presence. Cleanse me, oh Lord, yes, I'm in Your presence.

Give me the grace to forgive others who sin against me. Lord Jesus Christ, forgive me of my sins and release me from generational curses. In Jesus' mighty name I pray, Amen.

Prayers using Scripture

Lord Jesus Christ, forgive me my sins. With the staff of Moses, I divide and scatter every evil attack in my life, in my family's life, and in my home. God's mercy and favor are the architects of my heart, my family's heart, and my home. Satan, try me and try God!

Lord Jesus Christ, with the staff of Moses, I divide and scatter all the plans of our enemies. Elohim is in charge of my heart and of my home. As we go in and out, therefore, Satan is not permitted.

Elohim has come to protect my heart, my house, my family, my business, and supply all of our needs. In Jesus Christ's name I pray, Amen.

Praying in the Spirit

Father God, I bind every spirit of death hovering around my life and my family's life in the mighty name of Jesus Christ. Amen.

I command every dead organ in my body and in my family members' bodies to jerk back to life now, in the name of Jesus Christ. Amen.

I reject every spirit of death and the grave, in Jesus' name. Amen.

I declare supernatural restoration of everything I have lost in my life, in the name of Jesus. Amen.

Father, let Your creative power operate freshly in my entire body and in my family's body systems. In Jesus Christ's name I pray. Amen.

Father God, let the fire of the Holy Spirit enter my bloodstream and my family's bloodstream, and cleanse our systems in the name of Jesus Christ. Amen.

I command every evil plantation in our lives to come out with all your roots, in the name of Jesus Christ. Amen.

Evil strangers in our bodies and wombs, come all the way out of your hiding places, in the name of Jesus Christ. Amen.

Let all negative deposits circulating in our bloodstreams be flushed out by the blood of Jesus Christ. We are covered by the blood of Jesus.

Holy Ghost fire, burn from the top of our heads to the soles of our feet, in Jesus Christ's name. Amen.

Submit to God

Devil, I am resisting you, and you will flee from me and my family.

Thank You, Father God, that I can come before You with clean hands and a pure heart. I submit myself completely to You, giving thanks because as we draw near to You, You come closer and closer to us.

I praise You, Father, that I have power not only to resist the devil but to chase him away completely. He has to flee before Your power.

No longer will I be double-minded with wavering and divided interests, but I shall be single-minded, desiring only to serve and love You.

The devil can't touch me or my family. In Jesus Christ's name, Amen.

Decree and Declare

I decree and declare my days will be filled with joy, unspeakable joy and full of glory, the windows of heaven are open and supernatural wind are blowing hidden treasures into my life. I will reap undeniable fruit that no man can deny, God will not fail me, every repeated struggle in my life must end, its time is up today. All my battles will bow their knees and be burned by Holy Ghost Fire. The peace of God will reign in Jesus name, Amen.

God is Greater than Your Heart

From the end of the earth will I cry unto thee, when my heart is overwhelmed: lead me to the rock that is higher than I. Psalm 61:2

PRAYER

Father, right now my heart is burdened and overwhelmed within me, but I thank you, Lord, that even here you are greater for me. lead me to the rock that is higher than all that I feel, see or understand. Let all that is holding me lead me straight back to you and never away from you. In Jesus' name, amen.

God Over Fear

When I am afraid, I put my trust in you. In God, whose word I praise, in God I trust; I shall not be afraid. what can flesh do to me?
Psalm 56:3-4

PRAYER

Lord in all my fear I will not drown. Today, I put my trust in you. you are the God who cannot fail and who will not fail me. I will praise you all the more when I am afraid, for you are the God who is greater than all flesh. thank you that my fear will not overcome me, because it cannot overcome you. in Jesus' name, amen.

God of Strength

And he said to me, "My grace is sufficient for you, for My strength is made perfect in weakness." therefore most gladly I will rather boast in my infirmities, that the power of christ may rest upon me. 2 corinthians 12:9

PRAYER

My Lord and my God, thank you for your grace that is more than sufficient for all of my weaknesses. thank you for every limitation within me that leads me to rely on you and your strength made available for me. you have made me with this weakness that I may know through them your power that rests upon me. because of your grace, I'am not overcome but I have overcome. In Jesus' name, Amen.
PAGE 50

God as Your Secret Place

He that dwelleth in the secret place of the most high shall abide under the shadow of the almighty. Psalm 91:1

PRAYER

Father, thank you that I'am hidden in You; that I'am safe and kept in You, because You are my shelter, my covering, my watchman, and my keeper, I have rest in You and You alone, You are my fortress, and my refuge in whom I have placed my trust. with You, I'am secure. In Jesus' mighty name, amen.

God of Hope

Now the God of hope fill you with all joy and peace in believing, that ye may abound in hope, through the power of the Holy Ghost. Tomans 15:13.

PRAYER

Lord Jesus, You are the God of hope, and all my hope is found in You. Regardless of what it seems, hope in me will remain steadfast, for You will not fail me or cause me to be put to shame. Holy Spirit fill me with your joy and your peace, that my hope would continually abound and that I may see your goodness in every thing to do with me. In Jesus' mighty name, amen.

I command every evil arrow—Arrows of setback, arrows of failure, arrows of barrenness, arrows of frustration, arrows of sickness, arrows of disappointment, arrows of shame—that the enemy has fired at me, my business, and my family to return back to the sender, in the mighty name of Jesus.

Traveling Prayer

Dear Lord,
Please watch over and protect me as I embark on my journey. Be my guide and lead me safely to my destination. Surround me with your love and shield me from harm. Grant me the wisdom and clarity to make the right decisions while traveling. Help me to stay calm and alert, and to navigate any challenges that may arise. Bless the pilots, drivers, and all those responsible for my safe travels. May they be skilled and focused, and may your hand be upon them as they transport me to where I need to go.

I entrust myself into your care, knowing that you are always with me. Thank you for your constant presence and protection. In Jesus name...
Amen

PSALM 91

Those who live in the shelter of the Most High will find rest in the shadow of the Almighty.

This I declare about the Lord:

He alone is my refuge, my place of safety; he is my God, and I trust him.

For he will rescue you from every trap and protect you from deadly disease. He will cover you with his feathers.

He will shelter you with his wings.

His faithful promises are your armor and protection.

Do not be afraid of the terrors of the night, nor the arrow that flies in the day. Do not dread the disease that stalks in darkness, nor the disaster that strikes at midday.

Though a thousand fall at your side, though ten thousand are dying around you, these evils will not touch you. Just open your eyes, and see how the wicked are punished. - If you make the Lord your refuge, if you make the Most High your shelter, no evil will conquer you;

no plague will come near your home.

For he will order his angels to protect you wherever you go.

They will hold you up with their hands so you won't even hurt your foot on a stone. You will trample upon lions and cobras;

you will crush fierce lions and serpents under your feet!

The Lord says, "I will rescue those who love me.

I will protect those who trust in my name.

When they call on me, I will answer;

I will be with them in trouble.

I will rescue and honor them.

I will reward them with a long life and give them my salvation."

Daily Confession

I am forgiven of all sins.
I am healed of all diseases.
I am living a redeemed life.
I am sanctified by Truth.
I am God's beloved child.
I am perfected by Love.
I am full of joy.
I have no need.
I am bought by Your blood Lord Jesus.
I belong to You, not myself.
I am Your vessel Most High God.
I am loved by Jesus.
I am loved by my Father God.
I am loved by Holy Spirit.
I have a future and hope in You.
I will fulfill my destiny.
I hear my good Shepherd's voice.
I do not follow a stranger's voice.
I am surrounded by You, Love.
I walk by faith not by sight.
I am the righteousness of Christ.
I owe no one anything but to love them.
I love my brothers and sisters in Christ.
I walk in righteousness, peace and joy.
I am surrounded by favor

Weapons of Warfare Prayer

Father in heaven, I come before you in the mighty name of Jesus. I praise you for your power and great glory. I declare that your name is Jehovah-Gibowr the Lord who is mighty in battle. You are Jehovah-Sabaoth, the Lord of Hosts. I suit up with the armor of God, the helmet of salvation, the breastplate of righteousness, the belt of truth, my feet, they are shod with the preparation of the gospel of peace. I take up the shield of faith, which quenches every fiery dart of the wicked one and the sword of the Spirit which is the Word of God, I also take up the garments of vengeance and the cloak of zeal. I surround myself, my family with a smoke screen, acting as a sight and sound barrier against satanic agents, interlopers, and evil spirits. I identify the evil spirits and satanic agents that have taken up assignments against my home, family, business, and economy. I speak that the weapons of my warfare are not carnal but mighty in God to the tearing down of strongholds, the casting down of arguments and of every high thing which exalts itself against the knowledge of Christ. There are more with us than there are with them, I declare that your angels hearken unto the voice of your word, Therefore, I arm your angelic armies with your word and loose carnage against the enemy that has surrounded me, persecuted me, opposed me, and resisted me. I release arrows, lightnings, hailstones, and coals of fire, I scatter the enemies that have gathered themselves against Me My Family, with famine And devouring storms. I engage the spirits that have assembled from underwater locations and speak a sea quake. I speak that they are trapped in prisons assembled round about them locking them into pocket realms characterized by dry wind. I call for the drying up of the enemy's waters. I release engines of war, instruments of war, and instruments of death, upon the agents and devices of darkness in the name of Jesus. I choose to tread upon serpents and scorpions. The evil agents must be smitten by the rod of iron. loose the battle axe of God, into the encampments of darkness and target obstacles at their roots. The choirs and harmonies of darkness will suffer at the release of the blast of God and the rebuke from the voice of the Most High. I am a Born of God and an ambassador of heaven. I was not put here to suffer bullying at the hands of a defeated kingdom. I spite my enemies and exalt the name Jesus, the name that is above every name, at whose name every knee must bow in heaven and on earth and under the earth, I set fire the to the enemy's strategies with the fiery stream of God. I plant snares and traps on every evil assignment against my life calling them booby trapped. Ravenous birds devour wondrously in the encampments of darkness, Locusts devour the evil words and curses spoken against me, my house, destiny, business, ministry and everything under my stewardship. I engage with the heavenly bodies and employ the stars, declaring that just as the stars fought from their courses against Sisera, so the stars are deployed in agendas to advance the government of God in heaven and on the earth. I am more than a conqueror in Christ. I declare that as I move out of fear, for perfect love cast out fear, fear of the day and fear of the night is overtaking the governments of evil in the spirit realm. Tempest, strike the evil powers and do not relent. Deep sleep overtake the enemies that are fleeing, impaling them in their efforts to escape such that they feel the full impact of their rebuke. I declare portals, wormholes and escape routes are shut down in every realm, age, timeline, dimension, frequency, and vibration, past, present and future to infinity. May the warhorses of heaven tread down those that rise up against the name of Jesus Christ and the power of His might. I declare a massive clearing in the spiritual atmosphere and environment of my life and those connected to me and thank you, God Most High, that you came to punish the hosts of the high ones on high and the kings of the earth, Amen.

Trust in God's Provision
(In the AM)

Proverbs 3:5-6 (NIV) - "Trust in the Lord with all your heart and lean not on your own understanding; in all your ways submit to him, and He will make your paths straight."

Psalm 34:10 (NIV) - "The lions may grow weak and hungry, but those who seek the Lord lack no good thing."

Matthew 7:11 (NIV) - "If you, then, though you are evil, know how to give good gifts to your children, how much more will your Father in heaven give good gifts to those who ask him!"

Isaiah 41:10 (NIV) - "So do not fear, for I am with you; do not be dismayed, for I am your God. I will strengthen you and help you; I will uphold you with my righteous right hand."

Psalm 23:1 (NIV) - "The Lord is my shepherd, I lack nothing."

Decree
(In the AM)

"I decree that I am a blessed and prosperous child of God. I walk in the favor of the Lord, and He opens doors of financial abundance before me." (Deuteronomy 28:8)

"I decree that I am a faithful tither, and as I bring my tithes into the storehouse, God pours out blessings upon me and rebukes the devourer for my sake." (Malachi 3:10-11)

"I decree that God supplies all my needs according to His riches in glory. I trust in His provision and have no lack in any area of my life." (Philippians 4:19)

"I decree that I am a wise steward of my finances. I manage my resources with integrity, wisdom, and generosity, and I experience an increase in all that I set my hands to." (Luke 16:10)

"I decree that God has given me the power to create wealth. I walk in His divine wisdom and strategies, and I prosper in all my endeavors." (Deuteronomy 8:18)

Breaking Patterns in My Finances
(Upon Waking & Before Going to Sleep)
(Stay Consistent Until God Breaks All Patterns in Your Life)

Heavenly Father,
I come before You in the powerful name of Jesus Christ, my Lord, and Savior. I recognize that there may be negative spiritual influences and strongholds affecting my finances, and I surrender them to You today. I repent for any sins, known or unknown, that may have allowed these patterns to persist in my life. I ask for Your forgiveness, Lord, and I trust in Your grace to cleanse and renew me.

I put on the full armor of God as described in Ephesians 6:10-18. I take up the helmet of salvation, the breastplate of righteousness, the belt of truth, the shoes of the gospel of peace, the shield of faith, and the sword of the Spirit, which is Your Word.

I now declare that no weapon formed against me shall prosper, and every tongue that rises against me in judgment shall be condemned (Isaiah 54:17).

In the name of Jesus, I rebuke and bind any demonic forces or spiritual strongholds that have been negatively affecting my finances. I command them to release their hold over my life and my resources right now.

I declare that I am a child of the Most High God, and I have authority over all powers of darkness. I plead the blood of Jesus over every area of my finances, covering them with Your divine protection.

Lord, I invite Your Holy Spirit to fill every corner of my financial life. Give me discernment and wisdom to make sound financial decisions that align with Your will.

Help me break free from any patterns of fear, doubt, or unbelief. I trust in Your provision, Lord, and I believe that You are my ultimate source of abundance. Fill me with faith to see beyond my current circumstances and to walk in the prosperity and freedom that You have promised in Your Word.

Thank You, Father, for hearing my prayer. I stand firm in faith, knowing that You are at work, breaking every chain, and bringing breakthrough into my finances. In Jesus' name, I pray. Amen.

3 | PRAYERS (Part II)

And my God will meet all your needs
according to the riches of his glory in Christ Jesus."
-Philippians 4:19

PRAYER FOR PROVISION

Heavenly Father,
I come before You, believing in the promise of Philippians 4:19.
You are my God, and I trust in Your abundance and provision.
Your Word assures me that You will meet all my needs, not according to my efforts, but according to the riches of Your glory in Christ Jesus.

Lord, I surrender my financial needs to You today. I bring before You my bills, my debts, and my desires for financial stability. I trust that You see them all.

In faith, I claim this promise for my life. Provide for me, Father, in ways that only You can. Open doors of opportunity, bless the work of my hands, and guide me towards financial wisdom and stewardship.

Help me to lean on Your provision, not my own understanding. I choose to trust in Your timing, even when circumstances seem uncertain. Thank You for being my faithful provider. In Jesus' name, I pray.
Amen.

3 | PRAYERS (Part III)

Remember to Stay Consistent with Prayers from Part 1-3
Until God Breaks All Curses

PRAYER FOR FINANCIAL BREAKTHROUGH

Heavenly Father,
I come to You today, seeking a financial breakthrough in my life. You are the God of abundance and provision, and I believe that You have great plans for my financial well-being.
I surrender my financial worries, debts, and limitations to You, I release any fear or doubt that hinders me from fully trusting in Your faithfulness. I choose to place my faith in Your promises and provision.
Lord, I ask for Your wisdom and guidance in managing my finances. Help me make wise decisions, sow seeds of generosity, and be a faithful steward of what You have blessed me with. Open doors of opportunity and bring forth divine connections that will lead to financial increase. Break every chain of lack and scarcity in my life, and replace it with an abundance mindset rooted in Your Word. Renew my mind and align my thoughts with Your truth about prosperity and provision.
I declare that my financial breakthrough is on the way. I believe that You are working behind the scenes, orchestrating circumstances and aligning resources for my benefit. I trust in Your perfect timing and Your divine plan for my financial well-being.

Thank You, Lord, for Your unfailing love and care. I receive Your financial breakthrough with gratitude and praise. May Your name be glorified through my testimony of Your provision and blessings.
In Jesus' mighty name, I pray. Amen.
Be Blessed.

Important Instructions

Do not move forward until all is well with your financial life—until all patterns have ended and all curses have been broken.

If you want to be a business owner, or if you want increase in your business, if you want promotions, or if you have a dream job you've been praying and hoping for—God will do it for you after breaking all that was hindering your financial life. (Trust God.)

Congratulations,

I am thanking God for coming through for you, as I believe in our living, faithful, powerful, loving, Almighty God. I am saying congratulations because I am certain that God has done it for you, just as He did it for me.

As I was about to finalize this, it came to my heart to testify of how God gave me victory over the enemy—how God came through for me. While praying and confessing daily (Parts 1-3), morning and night, I was trusting God with all my being, knowing there is not one thing my God can't do.

One night, I went to sleep and God took me into a deep revelation. I found myself at one of my mom's cousin's houses—the one we used to visit often. As I looked inside the front patio, I saw my white purse—the one I was currently using every day—lying on the ground. The purse was open, and there was a long line of ants going in and out of it. In the revelation, I happened to see a red can of Raid (insect killer). I grabbed the Raid, sprayed it, and killed all the ants inside my purse.

God gave me victory at last.

A couple of weeks later, I began questioning God: What should I do? Where should I start? At the time, I was driving for Uber Eats. I was tired. I was weary. But God answered. Yes—He answered me while I was driving.

I had always wanted to be a business owner. God granted me just that. Now I am a business owner—everything I ever wanted and exactly how I imagined it. I now sit at home daily while I make money. My needs are met. My bills are paid. I am helping others in need—all for God's glory.

And God continues to increase me. This book—yes, the one God has assigned me to write for you reading this right now—is a big part of God continuing to work in my financial life. He is giving me financial freedom and using me to impact future generations in my family.

Most importantly, God wants to set His children free. He wants to release His children from all generational curses—especially His chosen ones. I am one of God's chosen. I had to go through the process. It was hard, but it doesn't have to be hard for you. God is using me to write this book so that you don't have to suffer through the same process.

All you need is consistency and faith.

Now, I will give you up to four prayers to pray over your finances—for God's protection over all that He has given you financially. Never lack in praying over your financial life.

3 | PRAYERS (Part IV)

And my God will meet all your needs according to the riches of his glory in Christ Jesus."
-Philippians 4:19

PRAYERS FOR FINANCIAL PROTECTION

1. *"Heavenly Father, In the name of Jesus, I rebuke any attack of the enemy on my finances. I declare that You are my provider and protector, and I trust in Your abundant provision. Shield me from any schemes or attacks that seek to hinder my financial breakthrough. May Your angels encamp around me, guarding and preserving my financial well-being. I stand firm in Your promises and resist every form of financial oppression or lack. Thank You for Your love and protection. In Jesus' name, I pray. Amen."*

Remember, God is with you, and He cares for every aspect of your life, including your finances. As we pray and stand on His promises, we can find peace and assurance in the face of any challenge. Wishing you a blessed day!

2. *"I renounce every negative word or curse spoken over my finances, whether by myself or others. These words hold no power, for I am a child of the Most High God, walking in His abundance."*

3. My thoughts and beliefs about finances align with God's Word. I cast down negative thoughts of lack and meditate on His promises of provision and blessing.

I break free from fear, doubt, and insecurity regarding my financial future, trusting in Your divine plan. You are my ultimate provider, and I place my faith in Your promises.

I commit to generosity, sharing blessings with others in need, knowing that as I give, it shall be given unto me.

I embrace financial stewardship, recognizing all I have belongs to You. I manage my resources with integrity.

I set clear financial goals and follow practical steps, trusting Your guidance and open doors of opportunity.

Thank You for breaking the spirit of poverty off my life, releasing me into financial freedom and abundance.

I am blessed to be a blessing, and Your goodness follows me always. In Jesus' name, I pray. Amen.

4. Prayer for Becoming the First Millionaire in Your Family

Heavenly Father, I lift myself up to You, as I dream of being the first millionaire in my family. I trust in Your abundant provision and Your desire to bless Your children with prosperity.

Lord, I pray for a divine breakthrough in my financial journey. May I experience a transformation that not only blesses my life but also impacts future generations in my family.

In the mighty name of Jesus, I declare and decree that I will be the first millionaire in my family. I release Your favor, wisdom, and opportunities for wealth creation into my life.

Break every chain of financial limitation and lack that has been passed down in my family. I declare a new legacy of abundance and prosperity for me and the generations to come.

Guide me in my financial decisions. Grant me discernment, creativity, and divine strategies to increase my income, build wealth, and be a blessing to others. As I experience financial success, keep my heart humble and generous. May I use my wealth to honor You, advance Your Kingdom, and be a light in the lives of others.

Thank You, Lord, for hearing this prayer. I believe and trust that You will fulfill Your promises. In Your abundant provision, I will become the first millionaire in my family, bringing glory to Your name.
In Jesus' name, I pray. Amen.

ABOUT THE AUTHOR

Lissa Thomas

Lissa Thomas is a child of the Most High God, chosen by Him. She has received God's Blessing that will change her life forever. "Now God has chosen me to share these prayers to help others tap in spiritually to be blessed and delivered and especially to be set free from financial attacks or curses."

www.ingramcontent.com/pod-product-compliance
Lightning Source LLC
Chambersburg PA
CBHW071415300426
44114CB00016B/2304